THE MYSTERY OF INIQUITY

IS WORKING SECRETLY AND UNDERGROUND TRYING TO DESTROY OUR FAMILY. IN FACT IS ALREADY AT WORK IN OUR FAMILY BLOODLINE [II THESS 2:7]

JAMES E. HARVEY

DENVER, COLORADO

Outskirts Press, Inc.
http://www.outskirtspress.com

ISBN: 978-1-4327-9778-2

Outskirts Press and the "OP" logo are trademarks belonging to Outskirts Press, Inc.

PRINTED IN THE UNITED STATES OF AMERICA

To my wife, Betty, who is the essence of love, a personal source of intercessory prayers, encouragement, and inspiration—and a cause for my passionate commitment for releasing my full potential in this book.
To my sons, Taj Harvey and James Harvey Jr., for their support.

God Changes the Times and **Seasons** . . .
Daniel 2:21–22 (KJV)

And he changeth the times and seasons; he removeth kings, and setteth up kings: he giveth wisdom unto the wise, and knowledge to them that know understanding.

He [God] revealeth the deep and secret things: he knoweth what is in the darkness, and the light dwelleth with him.

It's **Revival** Time!

This is the season for ALL **who** desire to be set free from bondage. This book is not only talking about your condition or problem . . .

But the Answer to
Your Deliverance!

ACKNOWLEDGMENTS

This book, *The Mystery of Iniquity*, tells how God revealed to me the secrets of defeating Satan and his legions of evil spirits and a unique way of how to break inherited and generational curses.

I want to thank my sister, Evangelist Loretta Bryant, and Missionary Annette Johnson for getting the book ready for publication. I also want to thank my church family, Soldiers of Jesus Christ Church, for prayers and support.

Most of all, I am grateful to God who has called me to share his information. I give all praise and honor and glory to God the Father, God the Son, and God the Holy Spirit.

Scripture References

Daniel 2:21–22 (KJV): And he changeth the times and seasons: he removeth kings, and setteth up kings: he giveth wisdom unto the wise, and knowledge to them that know understanding.

He [God] revealeth the deep and secret things: he knoweth what is in the darkness, and the light dwelleth with him.

This is the season for the African American and everybody who is reading this book and for all races of peoples. This is the season for us to get our bloodlines cleansed from iniquities and generational curses—filled with the Holy Ghost. This is the season for deliverance. This is the season for us to get in position for restoration. This is the season for us to cry out to the Lord of Saboath, which is the Master Avenger, The Lord of Hosts (James 5:4). This is the season for us to get back all that the devil stole from us, from your parents, from your great-grandparents.

Right now, just begin to decree, "The latter and former rain, prosperity, and abundance come to me now, in Jesus' name" (concerning restoration for African Americans, read the chapter on that subject).

The vision and the footnotes scripture on that Rhema Word I received:

Romans 5:20 (KJV): Moreover the law entered, that the offense might abound. But where sin abounded, grace did much more abound.

Romans 5:20–21 (KJV Living Bible): God's law was given so that all people could see how sinful they were. But as people sinned more and more, God's wonderful grace became more abundant. So just as sin ruled over all people and brought them to death, now God's wonderful grace rules instead, giving us right standing with God and resulting in eternal life through Jesus Christ our Lord.

Romans 5:20–21 (Today's English Version): Law was introduced in order to increase wrongdoing, but where sin increased God's grace increase much more. So, then, just as sin ruled by means of death so also God's grace rules by means of righteousness, leading us to eternal life through our Lord.

Romans 5:20–21 (The Message Bible): All that passing laws against sin did was produce more lawbreakers. But sin didn't, and doesn't, have a chance in competition with the aggressive forgiveness we call grace. When it's sin verses grace, grace wins hands down. All sin can do is threaten us with death, and that's the end of it. Grace, because God is putting everything together again through the Messiah [Jesus], invites us into a life—a life that goes on and on and on, world without end.

Romans 5:20–21 (The New American Bible): The law came in order to increase offenses but despite the increase of sin, grace has far surpassed it. So that, as sin reigned through death, grace may reign by way of justice leading to eternal life, through Jesus Christ our Lord.

Romans 5:20–21 (Amplified Bible): But then Law came in, [only] to expand and increase the trespass [making it more apparent and exciting opposition]. But where sin increased and abounded, grace (God's unmerited favor) has surpassed it and increased the more and superabounded, So that [just] as sin reigned in death, [so] grace (His unearned and undeserved favor) might reign also through righteousness (right standing with God) which issues in eternal life through Jesus Christ (the Messiah, the Anointed One) our Lord.

FOREWORD

Information is necessary, but our life will not change until we get a revelation of that information. When you get a revelation concerning certain things, it will not leave you. You can hear information from all around the world, but until the light comes on and a connection is made, it will profit you nothing.

Revelation takes us only halfway there; experience leads us all the way. The great tragedy is if you don't move into experience, the revelation remains locked in your mind and you think it's active in your life. In reality, hearing without doing has locked you into a form without power.

When God reveals things to us, we must put those things to work. If we don't, we will lose the power and opportunity that has been offered to us. Jesus warns us in Matthew 13:19, "When any one heareth the word of the kingdom, and understandeth it not, then cometh the wicked one, and catcheth away that which was sown in his heart. This is he which received seed by the wayside." (KJV).

My wife and I have been copastors of a church for 17 years. We are committed and have not traveled much. However, we bought several books on curses, iniquity, and deliverance. The ministry has experienced ups and downs. There have been many miracles, but no steady growth in membership. People came and received deliverance but did not stay. On one occasion after my wife had stayed up all night in prayer, God spoke through her concerning transportation, saying, everyone that needed a vehicle would receive it. The next day, they went and possessed their vehicles. A man with stage four cancer was instantly healed by the power of God. Demons were cast out and marriages were healed. But, in spite of all this, these individuals left the ministry and went to a church that did not believe in the supernatural. We began seeking God, asking him what was happening.

One morning I felt an urge to go to the church alone. I was low in spirit and had no energy. With my body in despair, I lay on the floor and just went to sleep. Although I was weak, I felt peaceful. Then God spoke to me. "Get up, get up! I allowed the people to leave your ministry so that you can seek me wholeheartedly regarding the work that I have called you to do. In 2008, I instructed you to write a book. You failed to do so. I had to get your attention."

I began to feel strength returning to my body, and the spirit of self-pity began to lift. God spoke again saying, "If you write this book as I have instructed you, your obedience will cause an impartation of my anointing to abide on you and in you. You will know when that time has come."

Therefore, I write this book as I was instructed to. However, before you attempt to share this information with others, read it cover to cover until you get a revelation. Of course, look it up in the Bible to see that it is so. Then begin to ask God to give you insight on the materials you have read.

Introduction

In the year of 2008, I was conducting a revival service for a good friend of mine. It was a three-night service and I was introducing "How to break generational curses." On the second day, the Holy Spirit woke me up early that morning and began to speak to me about African Americans and generational curses. He said that the reason Satan plagues this particular race is because the next people to experience the outpouring of his *Holy Spirit* will be among people of color. Satan has launched his attack in the form of:

- rebellion
- violence
- black-on-black crime
- drugs
- lack of self-worth

God said he is sending me primarily to the race of African Americans but not limited to people of color, because all races are suffering from generational curses. The root of these curses is iniquity. I want you to begin saying repeatedly *"but where sin abound, grace did much more abound."* The time will come when you will feel the sensation of running water. This is my anointing to bring forth deliverance in Jesus' name.

TABLE OF CONTENTS

CHAPTER 1
INTRODUCTION

Mystery—Something that is secret, hidden, or unexplained or something not known or not understandable.

When the Holy Ghost instructed me to write this book on *Mystery of Iniquities*, I began to mediate on racism, how white Americans (born-again believers) travel to the third world and give their whole life to serve people of color, then come back to the United States and face that spirit of racism and find themselves at the time walking in this mystery of iniquities. In this case it is racism. The reason that whites and African Americans face racism most of the time is because we have an enemy called Satan who wants to continue to divide. If he can keep us divided, he can conquer us all the time. White American bloodlines need to be cleansed completely by confession of this iniquity, repent, and apply the blood of Jesus. Brothers and sisters, you need to get this revelation. The devil doesn't care if you are saved or holding a high position in life.

These generational curses must be completely dealt with. The question always comes up when racism has taken place, and white Americans will come on television or radio and interview people of color and ask, "Will we ever move on? Slavery occurred a long time ago. Why have we not moved forward?" The reason is spiritual: our bloodline needs to be cleansed. The mystery of iniquities is something that is hidden or unexplained. Understand this: just because slavery took place before our time, demons and spirits don't die because your daddy, or grandfather, or great-grandfather has died. The spirit of racism must be dealt with in the whole race and the individual.

If the Holy Spirit permits me to write another book, I believe it will be for everybody. But you can get deliverance from this book. I am just being obedient. The Holy Spirit has instructed me to go to primarily people of color.

But I am not limited to people of color, because all races, all people, are facing this mystery of iniquities.

You have to remember, iniquities occur when they are practiced over and over again. In this case, racism is continuing from to generation and generation. You see that so-called Jim Crow laws have deceived many white Americans thinking that they are above African Americans. Jim Crow laws introduced the idea that African Americans are always second-class citizens who are not equal to white Americans. You can see that spirit is very much alive today. Willie Lynch is still alive to promote fear, distrust, and envy regarding African Americans in so many ways. You do not have to be a Christian to see the manifestation of this curse, because the division exists among African Americans and white Americans. This is 2011, and the first African American president of the United States is in office, and we have seen the Willie Lynch and Jim Crow spirits in operation. My next book will provide more details of this.

II Thessalonians 2:7 (KJV) states: For the mystery of iniquity doth already work: only he who now letteth will let, until he be taken out of the way.

KJV The Living Bible:
For this lawlessness is already at work secretly, and it will remain secret until the one who is holding it back steps out of the way.

Amplified Bible:
For the mystery of lawlessness (that hidden principle of rebellion against

constituted authority) is already at work in the world [but it is] restrained only until he who restrains is taken out of the way.

New International Version:
For the secret power of lawlessness is already at work; but the one who now holds it back will continue to do so till he is taken out of the way.

Wow! It's time for the church, the body of Christ, to set the captive free. This mystery of iniquity or spirit of lawlessness the Bible says is already at work, and it is time for the body of Christ to gather in the harvest. You need this revelation. As long as the church is here, the man of lawlessness (antichrist) can not come on the scene because we will have power over him, and he can not deceive many. Why? Grace and truth are here. The Holy Spirit is here. And most of all, Jesus Christ has delegated his full authority to his body (church), as well as binding and loosing (Matthew 16:19) and casting out demons (Mark 16:15–20).

But, my brothers and sisters, this is the time to prove the will of God.

The mystery of iniquity is already working in our family bloodline, in secret with power, causing our people, African Americans, to kill one another, do drugs, rebel, and act in violence, and we as the body of Christ have the answer. It's time to call this spirit of (lawlessness) iniquity to be broken off of our people so they can recover themselves from the snare of the devil (II Timothy 2:26).

This mystery of iniquity is also working in the white American family blood-line, causing an increase in racism, suicides, stealing, sexual perversion, pride, murder, superior feelings, thinking they are always right, and so forth. Not all white Americans are racist, but the mystery of iniquity has the ability some-times to overshadow a great majority of white Americans.

For example, Affirmative Action was designed to give African Americans an equal opportunity. However, some white Americans think African Americans only want a free handout. They are unaware that their motive is selfish. All African Americans want is an equal opportunity.

Colin Powell stated he thanked God for Affirmative Action, because without it, he would never have had the opportunity to be a general in the United States of America. In this book, we, as the body of Christ, are going to learn how to defeat the enemy and walk in total victory, treating everybody as you want to be treated. May this book fulfill the many questions you have asked yourself.

Why this is a must-read book: to walk in total victory, you must embrace and walk in the truth of God's Word.

Jeremiah 5:25 (KJV):
Your iniquities have turned away these things, and your sins have withholden good things from you.

KJV Living Bible:
Your wickedness has deprived you of these wonderful blessings. Your sin has robbed you of all these good things.

Proverbs 28:13 (KJV):
He that covereth his sins shall not prosper: but whoso confesseth and forsaketh them shall have mercy.

KJV Living Bible:
People who cover over their sins will not prosper but if they confess and forsake them, they will receive mercy.

John 9:31 (KJV)
Now we know that God heareth not sinners, but if any man be a worshipper of God, and doeth his will, him he heareth.

KJV Living Bible:
We know that God doesn't listen to the sinners, but he is ready to hear those who worship him and do his will.

There are two masters in this world: Jesus Christ and Satan. There are two kingdoms:

A. Kingdom of Light (Jesus Christ)
B. Kingdom of Darkness (Satan)

When you're born-again, letting Jesus Christ of Nazareth be Lord of your life, then and only then your master is Jesus Christ.

You can't demand anything if you are a sinner, because iniquity and sin will keep you in bondage. God don't know you, but you can, right now, ask Jesus to come into your life. Don't let religion stop you from seeing the truth. It is just the grace of God that God's blessing comes over the sinner. Now is the time to get serious. Let Jesus Christ be the Lord of your life.

Forget about that crazy slogan, "I am going to remain in my church the rest of my life." That sounds like a Christian, but it is religious; it's not of God. If you're going to make a statement, make this one: "Nay, in all these things we are more than conquerors through him that loved us. For I am persuaded, that neither death, nor life, nor angels, nor principalities, nor powers, nor things present, nor things to come, Nor height, nor depth, nor any other creature, shall be able to separate us from the love of God, which is in Christ Jesus our Lord" (Romans 8:37–39, KJV). The Holy Ghost, I believe, enlightened me concerning generational curses and iniquities.

When you are saved, we are tri-beings: spirit, soul, body.

A. When we invite Jesus to come in our heart (spirit), that is the only part that is saved (spiritually), although Jesus died on the cross for the whole man.
B. Our body, which is still mortal, not immortal, is still subject to all curses and iniquities as before.
C. To be victorious, read Romans 12:1–2, and so, dear brothers and sisters, I plead with you to give your bodies to God.

Let them be a living and holy sacrifice, the kind he will accept when you think of what he has done for you. Is this too much to ask? Don't copy the behavior and customs of this world, but let God transform you into a new person by changing the way you think. Then, you will know what God wants you to do, and you will know how good and pleasing and perfect his will really is.

This is why we must use our faith in Jesus Christ to exercise our authority and break all curses and iniquities that are trying to attack us. Now, as a believer of Jesus Christ, neither Satan nor his servants have any legal right to enforce any curses on us. But we have to know how to break curses, cast out demons, and to walk in total victory. We must continue to fight the good fight of faith. We must locate our enemy (wrong thinking). We must locate our battlefield (our mind).

The word "insecurity" means: the state of being, not secure, not confident, not firm.

The word "inferiority" means: the state of feeling lower in position, stature, or value.

If you are going to walk in total victory, you must be able to locate your enemy and locate the battlefield. Your greatest enemy is wrong thinking, and the battlefield is your mind.

You may say, "I thought Satan was my greatest enemy." He is your enemy, but he has been defeated. If he can't get you to believe a lie, then he has no power over you at all. He is powerless to touch you if you have right, godly thinking. The strategy of Satan, which hasn't changed throughout history, is the same to get you to believe a lie to make you feel insecure and inferior. Then, as your emotions of insecurity and inferiority begin to work in your life, he will present to you another lie. He will show you something bad and convince you it is pleasant and desirable to remove your insecurity and your inferiority. Once you partake of his fruit, you then have again entered his trap and reinforced his control over your life.

Today, as African Americans, as a believer of Jesus Christ of Nazareth, we can begin breaking curses, iniquities in our life. Before we can begin tearing down the strongholds on our life, the Bible says that we are to have a "ready mind." That means that we are to have a mind that is open to the will of God for us, whatever that will may be. In this book, *The Mystery of Iniquity*, I am asking you search the scriptures to see that all this information is true (Acts 17:11–14). This book is for those that believe God for a turnaround in their life.

This calls for wholehearted commitment.

Isaiah 5:13 (KJV) states, Therefore my people are gone into captivity, because they have no knowledge.

Wow! This is our season. This is our time for the African American family bloodline to be cleansed from violence, drugs, black-on-black crime, murders (knowledge sets the captive free).

The principle thing (Proverbs 4:5, 7, KJV) is: Get wisdom, get understanding: forget it not . . . Wisdom is the principal thing; therefore get wisdom and with all thy getting get understanding.

We need to pray for wisdom and a discerning or hearing heart.

Everyone has questioned God at one time or another. Some people even get mad at God. But there is nothing to be gained by getting mad at God. A lack of knowledge causes you to accept things you thought God sent, when God was not responsible at all. It was the devil.

II Timothy 2:26 instructs us to remember that Satan gets his power through deception. God's people are destroyed for lack of knowledge.

Your body of authority, Jesus himself, said you have authority to bind evil from the earth. You are not binding it from the whole earth, but you can bind it from the part you walk on. However, you cannot bind it if you do not know you have the authority to do so.

As a believer, you need to realize that your body gives you authority on the earth. A spirit being must have a body in order to manifest itself in the earth. That is why Satan has no legal authority here. He does not have a physical body. That is also why he hates your body and why he wants you sick or crippled. He wants you to kill one another or be dead.

Satan has no authority on earth because he does not have a physical body. He had to borrow the body of a serpent to talk to Eve in the Garden. Deception is how he gets the authority to bring disaster.

Do it now. Begin now to bind out of your life the things that have already been bound out of heaven. Bind evil from your property; bind it out of your home. Loose to you walking in divine health, your home, your seed to be covered with the blood of Jesus.

Say what the Word of God says: *I decree I have the victory in every circumstance, because the blood of Jesus is over me, around me, in me, causing your servant to have victory in Jesus' name.* Begin worshipping Jesus and thanking him.

CHAPTER 2
THE MYSTERY OF INIQUITY

Now let us take a look at the word "iniquity," which means to bend or distort (the heart). It also implies a certain weakness, or predisposition, toward a certain sin. Isaiah says Christ was bruised for our iniquities. If you commit a certain sin once and repent of it and never do it again, then that's the end of it. However, your sin becomes an iniquity when you keep committing that same act. It goes from being a sin to an iniquity, something that is practiced over and over again until it becomes spontaneous. Given certain circumstances or the right environment, you will bend it in that direction.

If a sin is repeatedly committed, it becomes an iniquity which can be passed down through the bloodline. When a person continually transgresses the law, iniquity is created in him, and that iniquity is passed to his children. The offspring will have a weakness toward that same kind of sin. Each generation adds to the overall iniquity, further weakening the resistance of the next generation to sin.

> Thou shewest lovingkindness unto thousands,
> and recompensest the iniquity of the fathers into the
> bosom of their children after them; the Great, the Mighty God,
> the Lord of hosts, is his name.
> (Jeremiah 32:18, KJV)

There is a relationship between curses and the sins of the father. Not only are the children affected, but also the generations to come. Exodus 20:5 speaks very specifically about the iniquities of the forefathers. If the family tree is not cleansed of this iniquity, then each generation becomes worse and will do what their parents, grandparents, and great-grandparents did. The next generation will bend in the same way of the past generations, and it becomes a bond of iniquity, or generational curse, in that family.

We have all seen families where one or both parents or grandparents were alcoholics and one or more of the offspring became alcoholics too. And to think, it all started as a sin with that one person who overindulged, but because they practiced it and did not try to get free through godly repentance, their drinking became an iniquity. Consequently, that family begins to bend, or has a predisposition, toward alcoholism.

Another way to describe a life under a curse is the word "adversity." This includes adverse circumstances, misfortune, or continual struggles or difficulties.

> Moreover all these curses shall come upon thee,
> and shall pursue thee, and overtake thee, till
> thou be destroyed.
> (Deuteronomy 28:45, KJV)

Notice how curses operate. They come upon you. The first reaction is to try to get away from them. People do everything in their power to dodge them or escape from them. But a curse will pursue you. No matter where you turn, a curse will chase after you in order to overtake, capture, kill, or defeat you. The only remedy is to break it by being delivered from it.

Hallelujah! Jesus was bruised for my iniquities! His work on the cross was the provision I needed to change the tide of a generational curse and walk in total mental health and victory! He's done the same for you, too, through the wounds and bruises he endured on the cross—the provision has been made to restore you and your family to that state of blessedness Adam and Eve once enjoyed in the Garden.

The difference between a wound and a bruise is that if you wound yourself, it will eventually scab over and heal. A bruise, however, can stay around for a long time. It may become discolored and can even go so deeply as to bruise the bone. An iniquity can be likened to a bruise because it stays around and goes to the bone from generation . . . to generation . . . to generation.

Some of us know some things about the lives of our grandparents. Very few of us have any knowledge about our great-grandparents at all. In general, we know almost nothing about our family's history. If people followed God's Word, they would be diligently teaching their children the history of their own family, especially those things that God did in the lives of their ancestors—both blessings and curses. This loss of knowledge of family history seriously affects our lives. Because we are unaware of the curses inherited through our bloodline, we end up walking in the same sins as our forefathers and reaping the same troubles as a result.

The apostle Paul had a revelation of this when he wrote

> For the mystery of lawlessness is already at work; only
> He who now restrains will do so until He is
> taken out of the way (II Thessalonians 2:7, NAB).

The mystery of iniquity Paul is referring to is the unseen and mysterious connection between a father's sins and the path of his children. For example, if the father is a liar and thief, his children are prone to the same behavior, regardless of their training, social, culture, or environmental influences.

CHAPTER 3
CAN A BELIEVER STILL BE UNDER A CURSE?

Let us first give a biblical definition of a curse. What does the Word of God have to say about the subject of curses?

A curse is God's recompense in the life of a person and his or her descendants as a result of iniquity. The curse causes sorrow of heart and gives demonic spirits legal entry into a family, whereby they can carry out and perpetuate their wicked devices.

Iniquity is the cause of curses. Because of the iniquity of the fathers, children can be born under a curse. David stated that he was conceived in iniquity. Children conceived in adultery, fornication, drunkenness, rejection, and rape are especially vulnerable to demonic attack and open to various curses.

> Be not deceived; God is not mocked: for
> whatsoever a man soweth, that shall he also reap.
> (Galatians 6:7, KJV)

This scripture has puzzled many people, especially within the body of Christ. The most common question asked is, "I gave my life to Jesus. Why are my children suffering from the same sins I used to do? Am I being punished?"

... visiting the iniquity of the fathers upon the children unto the third
and fourth generation of them that hate me.
(Exodus 20:5b, KJV)

According to Jeremiah 32:18, the iniquity of the father is recompensed into the
bosom of their children. In other words, what the parents do will affect their
children. The curses not only affect them, but their descendants as well. The
curse will continue down the bloodline until it is stopped by repentance and
faith in the redemption provided by Christ through the cross.

So, the answer is, when you become a believer of Jesus Christ, you can stop
this cycle. As a believer in Jesus Christ, you can put a stop to the working of
the enemy in you life no matter how many generations it has been in operation.

> Christ has redeemed us from the curse of the
> law, having become a curse for us; for it is written,
> Cursed is everyone who hangs on a tree.
> (Galatians 3:13, KJV)

We are redeemed from the curse. In other words, Jesus became a curse in our
stead. If this is true, how can a believer still be under a curse? To understand
this, we need to know the difference between what is legally ours and what is
experientially ours.

Just because something is legally yours does not mean you will automatically
obtain it and walk in it. What makes this even truer in spiritual matters is the
fact that we have an adversary, the devil, who is determined to keep away from
us what is legally ours. If he can keep us ignorant, he can still enforce a curse
against you even though you are legally redeemed from it. The same is true in
the case of sickness and disease. Although the Word of God teaches that we
are already healed by the stripes of Jesus, there are many believers who have not
appropriated this promise and continue to battle with sickness. This is because
healing is a part of our redemption, but it is not automatic. Unfortunately, there
are still many believers living under a curse even though they have been legally

redeemed from it. Just as a believer may have to fight a good fight of faith for healing, they may also have to fight a good fight of faith against curses.

Korah rebelled against the leadership of Moses and Aaron. If you go back and study the family tree of Korah, you'll see he was assigned to be the worship leader for the tabernacle. His family tree was to produce worship and praise and was a part of the priestly family that took care of the tabernacle. God had a divine assignment for his family, but Korah decided he was more spiritual than Moses and Aaron, and that they shouldn't be leaders. He began to plant seeds of rebellion and caused others to rebel against Moses and Aaron. Moses did not retaliate; he prayed instead. After he prayed, God opened the ground and swallowed Korah.

What a shame. Korah and his family were destroyed because of pride and re-bellion (iniquity). However, not all of Korah's family was destroyed. His sons did not stand with him in his rebellion. They decided that just because their father was following the path of iniquity, it didn't mean they had to follow suit. In fact, if you follow their lineage, you'll discover that their descendants became worship leaders in the tabernacle and in Solomon's Temple, which was one of the seven wonders of the ancient world.

The prophet Daniel understood the mystery of iniquity and the principle of confession in order to receive deliverance. Daniel is described in the scriptures as being a very godly man, highly esteemed by God. He was called "beloved" of the Lord. He received the revelation of King Nebuchadnezzar's dream and was delivered by God from the lion's den.

Because he understood the mystery of iniquity, the sins of the fathers passed to future generations, he knew that Israel's 70 years of captivity were almost over. God had told them through Jeremiah that at the end of 70 years they would return to Jerusalem, rebuild the temple, and restore the land. However, the 70 years were almost over and there were no signs that their captivity was end-ing. Why? Because the iniquity of the nation had not been confessed, and the bloodline had not been cleansed. In other words, Daniel said, he knew he was a part of the iniquity that held them in bondage. Therefore, when he prayed, he included himself as being guilty of the national iniquity.

The Israelites did not see a turnaround in their situation until Daniel confessed the sins of his forefathers and the sins of the nation of Israel. Here are just a few verses of that prayer.

> "O Lord, according to all Your righteousness,
> I pray, let Your anger and Your fury be turned away from Your
> city Jerusalem. Your holy mountain;
> because for our sins, and for the iniquities of
> our fathers, Jerusalem and Your people are
> a reproach to all those around us.
>
> Now therefore, our God, hear the prayer of Your
> servant, and his supplications, and for the
> Lord's sake cause your face to shine on Your
> sanctuary, which is desolate" (Daniel 9:16–17, NKJV)

The Message Remix Bible

> "We confess that we have sinned, that we have lived bad
> lives. Following the lines of what you have
> always done in setting things right, setting
> people right, please stop being so angry with
> Jerusalem, your very own city, your holy mountain.
> We know it's our fault that this has happened, all
> because of our sins and our parents' sins, and
> now we're an embarrassment to everyone around
> us. We're a blot on the neighborhood. So
> listen, God, to this determined prayer of your
> servant. Have mercy on your ruined Sanctuary.
> Act out of who you are, not out of what we are."

The ninth chapter of Ezra also demonstrates prayer by the children of Israel, confessing the sins of their forefathers as well as their own sins. Ezra clearly understood the principle of the people wasting away in the iniquities of their fathers as well as their own iniquities. In Ezra's mind, the sins of the fathers and the sins of the children were very much linked together. Read the entire chapter. But, for the sake of time, let's look at Ezra 9:7

> Since the days of our fathers to this day
> we have been very guilty, and for our iniquities
> we, our kings, and our priests, have been delivered
> into the hand of the kings of the lands, to
> the sword, to captivity, to plunder, and to
> humiliation, as it is this day (NKJV).

The scripture shows that God always honored such prayers of repentance and brought revival and prosperity back to the nation of Israel. Through these prayers of confessing the sins of the forefathers, the curses were lifted off the people and the land.

Satan may not have a legal right to enforce a curse against you, but he is an outlaw and will attempt to do so anyway. Therefore, curses have to oftentimes be broken over the lives of believers, and they must learn how to stand in fight against those curses—keeping them from operating in their lives. The promises in the Word are not automatic. They must be believed, and often involve fighting. So, if you are a believer and you are experiencing the symptoms of curses, you will have to be loosed from them before you will be able to walk in the full blessings of Jesus Christ of Nazareth. Through Jesus Christ, the generational curse(s) that has held you and your family in bondage can be broken.

Daniel prayed three times a day and here is a model prayer for deliverance:

Father God, I come before you in the name and in the power of your Son, Jesus. I admit that I am a sinner, and I ask you to forgive me of all my sins. Jesus, come into my heart and make me a new person. Change me from the inside out and mold me into who you want me to be. Father, as you gave your Son's life for me, I give my life to you. Right now, I break every family curse and every generational curse on my life. I plead the blood of Jesus Christ over my mind, my spirit, and my body. I break every yoke and every bondage from my past, and I sever those ties through the power of the blood of Jesus. I declare my freedom right now. I claim my liberty right now. I claim all that has been lost to be restored to me right now. Fill me, Lord, with your love, peace, joy, and victory, in Jesus' name, amen.

CHAPTER 4

The Principle of Confessing Your Iniquity and the Iniquity of Your Father

A search of the Old Testament will show that every time there was a revival in Israel, the first thing the Hebrew nation did was confess the iniquities of their forefathers. Look at what the people did in Nehemiah's time. Nehemiah was sent by God to enable the people to rebuild the wall around Jerusalem. The people had fallen in sin. In fact, they had fallen into the very same sins that had resulted in their fathers and grandfathers being taken away into captivity just 70 years before. They needed a revival and the curse of judgment to be lifted from their lives. Look at what these people did. Nehemiah confessed the sins of his fathers. "O God!" he pleaded, "have mercy on us." He could have said, "I didn't do anything wrong, so I don't have to confess the things that they did." But, he recognized the mystery of iniquity at work in his bloodline and realized he had the same bend his fathers and the nation of Israel were guilty of. After Nehemiah's prayer, the king of Persia let him go back to rebuild the walls and the gates and made provision for building supplies. They finished building in 52 days and the most prosperous time that Israel had was the next 400 years. Why? Because if you cover your sins or the sins of your family, you will not prosper.

He that covered his sins shall not prosper.
But whoso confesseth and forsaketh them shall
have mercy (Proverbs 28:13, KJV).

But if you confess your sins, you will prosper. Nehemiah didn't try to cover or deny his family's national iniquities. Likewise, we need to humble ourselves and pray over the sins that have been committed in America. We need to include ourselves because that's when healing can come.

In Nehemiah, chapter 9:1–2, the entire congregation repented for their iniquities. God healed their land and cleansed them.

Now in the twenty and fourth day of this month
the children of Israel were assembled with
fasting, and with sackclothes, and earth upon them.
And the seed of Israel separated themselves from
all strangers, and stood and confessed their sins,
and the iniquities of their fathers (KJV).

CHAPTER 5

GENERAL PRAYERS

Jim Crow law, breaking the curse on African Americans.

Willie Lynch's speech, spoken word curse, causing division among African Americans.

If Satan has cursed you without legitimate right to do so, then use your keys.

If the curse is from Satan and he has the legal right to do so, these are the steps to take:

A. Personal items

B. Deliverance prayer to be set free

General Prayers
The blood of Jesus and the power of the cross, break those curses right now!

The curse is reversed:

A. Through the name of Jesus

B. Through the blood of Jesus

C. Through the cross of Jesus Christ

Deuteronomy 23:5 tells us that God will turn your curses into blessings, because he loves you.

Jesus just didn't take our sins, but he took the curse of the sin on the cross.

Jim Crow Curse on African Americans

The Jim Crow Laws

In this chapter, I am not going in full details about Jim Crow laws, but what they were designed to do.

The Jim Crow system's clear purpose was to offer constant and undeniable evidence that African Americans would be required by law to regard themselves as second-class citizens forever. Get this: *forever, forever*. The true aim was not just the separation of the races (that was the expressed intention), but the long-term social and psychological intimidation of African Americans (the unexpressed and still unspoken intention).

Obstacles and Opportunities

Don't assume that the term "Jim Crow" refers only to legal measures. As a practical matter, the term refers to both the formal and informal dimensions of the program (to deprive one of their rights as a citizen, of the right to vote, the Jim Crow curse on African Americans holding office, etc.). It involved discrimination and public humiliation of African Americans from the 1880s and in the South and elsewhere in the United States.

As I was reading on black history, the Holy Spirit started to enlighten me that this Jim Crow is a curse because it began with sin moving to iniquity continually down generation to generation. Because of this iniquity, I believe insecurity demons and inferiority demons had been unleashed on African Americans. But first I recommend breaking that Jim Crow curse, then commanding the demons of insecurity and inferiority to come out and be gone in Jesus' name.

Say it now:

In the name of Jesus Christ of Nazareth, we renounce every spoken word and curse that Jim Crow laws stated that African Americans will always be regarded as second-class citizens forever.

We as African Americans come with repentance in our heart and ask you, Heavenly Father, to forgive us. We repent of our iniquities, and we ask you to forgive our fathers' and our forefathers' iniquities as well. We as African Americans repent for receiving these Jim Crow laws in our bloodline as regarding ourselves as second-class citizens.

Jim Crow Curse on African Americans

Through the blood of Jesus and the power of the cross, we break the Jim Crow curse!

Now, in Jesus' name, repeat: By the blood of Jesus and the power of the cross, we command all demons, insecurity demons, inferiority demons, and all associated with this Jim Crow curse to go now!

Say it again.

Spoken Words Curses on African Americans

Spoken Words Curses on African Americans that causes division:

Willie Lynch's Speech on Slave Control

This speech was delivered by Willie Lynch, on the bank of the James River in the Colony of Virginia in 1712. Lynch was a British slave owner. There, the term "lynching" was derived from his last name. Are remnants of Willie's methods still in use today?

In my bag here, I have a full proof method of controlling black slaves. I guarantee of you, that if installed correctly, it would control the slaves for 300 years. My method is simple and members of your family and overseer can use it.

I have outlined a number of differences among the slaves . . . and make them bigger. I use fear, distrust, and envy, for control purposes. These methods have worked on my modest plantation in the West Indies and [they] will work through the South.

The second is "color" or "shade." There is intelligence, size, sex, size of plantation, status of plantation.

The black slaves, after receiving his indoctrination, shall carry on and will become self-refueling and self-generating for hundreds of years, maybe thousands.

Don't forget you must pitch the old black, versus the young black, and the young black male against the old black male. You must use the dark skin slaves, versus the light skin slaves, and the light skin slaves, versus the dark skin slaves.

You must also have your white servants and overseers distrust all blacks, but it is necessary that your slaves trust and depend on us. They must love, respect, and trust only us.

Gentlemen, this kit are keys to control. Use them. Have your wives and children use them. Never miss an opportunity. My plan is guaranteed and the good thing about this plan is that if used intensely for one year the slave themselves will remain perpetually distrustful.

The purpose for this material being in this book is to show the beginning of the roots of division among African Americans, from generation to generation. It became iniquity, then this curse came on us. These curses are still affecting us. White Americans still try to use these methods: fear, distrust, and envy for control purposes. These spoken word curses, causing by the mystery of iniquity, need to be broken *now* in our African American families. We need to break these curses that are destroying one another, causing us to envy one another and fear one another.

It's time for us to start trusting one another again.

Breaking the Spoken Word Curses
on African Americans

In the name of Jesus Christ of Nazareth, we renounce every spoken word curse of that Willie Lynch speech, spoken over African Americans, in the area of fear, distrust, and envy, in our bloodline.

We confess our iniquity, the iniquity of our fathers, and our forefathers. We, as African Americans, repent for receiving these negative words of fear, distrust, and envy in our bloodline. We ask you, Heavenly Father, please forgive our fathers' and forefathers' iniquity. We ask you, Father, for the blood of Jesus to cleanse our bloodline.

By the blood of Jesus and the power of the cross, we break these "Willie Lynch spoken word curses" that have been placed on African Americans. We break it *now* in Jesus' name!

By the blood of Jesus and the power of the cross, we command all demons and spirits associated with these curses—fear, distrust, envy—that cause division among ourselves to leave us now. Say *now*!

If Satan has cursed you without a legitimate right to do so, then use your keys.

Speak out loud, take authority of every iniquity and every curse in the name of Jesus Christ, and command it to be broken right now.

Command it to be broken right now! Say it: *By the blood of Jesus and the power of the cross, I break those curses—right now!*

(Demand it—say it—break it right now!)

By the blood of Jesus and the power of the cross, I command all demons and spirits, associated with this curse to leave me now.

If the curse is from Satan and he has the legal right to do so, these are the steps to take: Confess your iniquities and the iniquities of your fathers and forefathers and acknowledge the sin that gave Satan, and/or his servants the right to place the curse on you. Repent and ask God for forgiveness and cleansing.

The Use of Personal Items

Often, a less powerful witch or person involved in an occultic religion requires some personal possession or object before they can send a curse onto someone. They use these articles in their rituals to send the curses.

Common items used are photographs, pieces of hair or nail clippings, and personal articles of clothes. These are used as markers. The demon spirits involved in these types of rituals require such items to identify the person they are been sent to afflict.

When you realize that someone has taken an article belonging to you for the purpose of using it in a ritual to curse you, it is best to retrieve the object. This may be impossible but don't get discouraged. Our God is powerful, and he made provision for our deliverance regardless of this difficulty. We recommend that the person being cursed pray this prayer:

Father, in Jesus' name, I pray that you send warrior angels to destroy any such stolen personal articles and render them ineffective for demonic use.

By the blood of Jesus and the power of the cross, I break this curse—right now!

Say it again, break it right now.

By the blood of Jesus and the power of the cross, I command all demon spirits associated with this curse to leave me immediately in the name of Jesus!

CHAPTER 6

THE INIQUITIES AND CURSES UPON AFRICAN AMERICANS

Inherited Curses:

A. Something we inherited, an iniquity of our father and our forefathers. The good news is that we don't have to put up with those curses any more.

B. The principle of how to break these terrible cycles in the Word of God.

You shall perish among the nations, and the land of your enemies shall eat you up. And those of you who are left shall waste away in their iniquity in your enemies' lands; also in their fathers' iniquities, which are with them, they shall waste away. (Leviticus 26:38–39, NKJV).

The survivors waste away in the iniquities of their forefathers. How many people today are wasting away in the iniquities of their forefathers without realizing it? Whole nations are being destroyed because of the iniquities of the forefathers.

Let's look at a modern-day example. In the country of Rwanda in Africa, one tribe rose up against another and massacred thousands and thousands of people. The people of the oppressed tribe fled to camps in Zaire. There in the refugee camps, thousands more died of cholera. The rest of the world watched in horror and amazement as CNN filmed the whole spectacle. Then, the oppressed tribe came to power in Rwanda and began to massacre the first tribe.

A reporter who had visited the refugee camps of both tribes had written some fascinating articles. When he talked to the refugees, he asked them the same question repeatedly.

Now that the war in Rwanda has ended, do you think you can go back and live in peace with people of the other tribe?

Without exception, the answer was the same. "No. We can never live in peace with the other tribe until the blood of our slain people has been avenged." And so the vicious cycle continues. Wouldn't you think those people in the refugee camps would have learned by the terrible things they experienced that intertribal warfare has no benefits? But, they have not dealt with the sins of their fathers and forefathers. In Satan's kingdom, blood calls for blood, and the killing never stops.

The whole continent of Africa is characterized by tribal warfare. In 1995, uprisings of intertribal warfare and massacres occurred in Kenya as well. We have all seen the same thing in Somalia as it was filmed by the news media. The people of Africa have never broken away from the sins of their forefathers. Each tribe is consequently ruled by particular demon gods. Demons hate people and are determined to exterminate them. Thus, the whole history of Africa has been incessant warfare and massacres among tribes. Until the Christians unite as one body and cry out to God in repentance for the sins of demon worship and hatred and warfare among their tribes as well as their ancestors' tribes, the curses from the sins of their forefathers will not be removed from their lives. Christians and non-Christians alike are being killed in those massacres. They are wasting away in the iniquities of their fathers (Leviticus 26:39).

This same problem exists here in America. The biggest problem in any large city is gang warfare and violence. Most of this is black-on-black violence. Why?

Because the intertribal warfare among blacks is being carried on right here in America. Each gang is the same as a tribe. It doesn't matter that these precious people are no longer in Africa. They are still wasting away in the iniquities of their forefathers.

Will God send you to hell for the sins of your fathers and forefathers? No. However, their sins and the resultant curses will affect your life unless you deal with them through Jesus Christ. How do you separate yourself from the sins of your ancestors? By confession: clear acknowledgment of these sins as sin before God (1 John 1:9), and then asking the Lord to separate you completely from the sins of your ancestors.

The Principle of How to Break
These Terrible Cycles in His Word

Praise God! There is a solution—Jesus Christ died on the cross to pay the price for all of our sins. Also, God clearly explains the principles of how to break these terrible cycles in his Word.

If they shall confess their iniquity, and the iniquity of their fathers, with their trespass which they trespassed against me, and that also they were have walked contrary to me. (Leviticus 26:40, KJV)

And that I also have walked contrary to them and have brought them into the land of their enemies if their uncircumcised heart be humbled and they then accept of the punishment of their iniquity.

Then I will remember my covenant with Jacob, and my covenant with Isaac, and my covenant with Abraham, I will remember the land.

CHAPTER 7

BREAKTHROUGH PRINCIPLES OF PRAYER TO BE SET FREE

Revival Service

Deliverance Prayers for the African Americans

Restoration for African Americans

Let's Remove the Curses and Release the Blessings on African Americans

Revival Service
(Leviticus 26:40–42, KJV)
If they confess their iniquity, and the iniquity of their fathers, with their trespass which they trespassed against me . . . Then will I remember my covenant . . .

God has a covenant with all nations and his people who call on his name. If we as Christians will begin to repent for the iniquity that has crept into our nation, God will cause the minds of our people to become right again, and he will pour out his covenant blessing on America.

Yes, Jesus Christ is the burden-removing, yoke-destroying Saviour. He was wounded for our transgressions. His blood has set us free, but unless we

| 29

understand that his blood will also break the iniquity, or the curse, we will continue to fall into sin. Like the Jewish people in Daniel's day, through the power of the blood of Jesus we can be set free now. (Say *now*.)

God is saying to us as a nation "Repent." We can repent from what those who have gone before us brought into our nation. We can repent for the evil our nation has committed against God. We can repent for the iniquity that's holding our race (African Americans) or nation in bondage. Jesus wants to set all the captives free. We now understand the principle of confessing your iniquity and the iniquity of your fathers and forefathers.

Now we understand the **mystery of iniquity**, the sins of the fathers passed on to future generations. In Israel's time when Daniel confessed the sins of the nation's forefathers, there was a turnaround for the nation of Israel. He had to confess because the curse had to be lifted from their lives. We have to recognize the mystery of iniquity at work in our bloodline and realize we have the same genes our fathers and forefathers had. Our bloodline needs to be cleansed. LET'S BEGIN NOW!

In Nehemiah 9, the entire congregation repented for their iniquities and the iniquities of their **fathers and forefathers. Because of this, God healed** the land and cleansed them.

I believe as African Americans we need to do as Nehemiah, Daniel, and Ezra did for their people, the children of Israel. We need to repent for our iniquities and the iniquities of our fathers and forefathers in the areas of rebellion, violence, crime, black-on-black crime, drugs, hatred for God, etc. Let's believe in God for a complete turnaround of African Americans.

Deliverance Prayers for the African Americans

Father, in Jesus' name, we as African Americans confess our iniquities and the iniquities of our fathers and forefathers in the areas of rebellion, violence, black-on-black crime, drugs, hatred for God, etc.

We have sinned, and we come with repentance in our hearts asking you for forgiveness. We repent for our iniquities. We ask you to forgive our fathers' and our forefathers' iniquities. Father, have mercy on us. We're guilty of disobedience toward your commandments. Please grant us favor. Lift the curse of judgment off our lives. Father, we petition as **African Americans right now.** We declare that the iniquity on our race is broken locally and nationally through the power of the blood of Jesus. Broken off our family, broken off our community, broken off our city. These iniquities are broken off African Americans through the blood of Jesus.

We bind principalities of the rulers of darkness of this world's spiritual wickedness in high places. You are bound here on earth. And we loose the anointing of the Holy Spirit to set us free.

In the name of Jesus we take authority over the spirits of iniquity that are pressuring our people to kill one another, to be violent, rebellious, commit black-on-black crimes and do drugs. Tonight, we declare your power is broken off us through the power of the blood of Jesus Christ. We take authority over every family curse, every sin and curse that has come in our lives through these iniquities. We command it is broken off through the power of the cross of Jesus Christ. (Say "Free.") I am free to serve Jesus Christ as our Lord and Savior. Free to praise Jesus. Free to accept Jesus Christ as our personal savior. Say "I'm Free! Who the Son (Jesus) sets free is free indeed."

Begin to thank Jesus for the turnaround. The power of darkness is broken off African Americans. Praise him!

Restoration for African Americans

Indeed the wages of the laborers who mowed your fields, which you kept back by fraud, cry out; and the cries of the reapers have reached the ears of the Lord of Sabaoth (James 5:4, NKJV).

Here, crying aloud, are the wages you withheld from the farmhands who harvested your fields. The cries of the harvesters have reached the ear of the Lord of Hosts (The New American Bible).

The owners, the wicked businesses, have kept back some of the people's wages. Once again, I want to be careful not to leave you with the idea that all businesses, all owners, and all wealthy people are in this category. God is pointing out those who have become wealthy by defrauding the wage earners. Now, it is extremely important that you understand what God is saying here, because this is the key to the end-time transfer of wealth. The cries of the reapers (workers/laborers) have reached the ears of the Lord of Sabaoth. I think many times people mistakenly read this, the Lord the Sabbath. Leader of a great army or mass. The Lord of Sabaoth is the Master Avenger in the very last days when the Lord comes for his glorious bride, who will be in no poverty or sickness. We will cry out to the Master Avenger, and he will take the wealth from the wicked, those who have kept back wages by fraud, and put it into the hands of the righteous.

Israel, when they came out of Egypt, is our example. Have you ever wondered why Israel left Egypt with all the silver and gold, all the wealth of Egypt? The reason is that after 400 years, they called on the Lord of Sabaoth, the Master Avenger. When he delivered them, not in the Promised Land, but on the way to the Promised Land, he brought them out and he caused the Egyptians to put silver and gold into their hands because they owed them 400 years' worth of back wages. This was a fine example of the wealth of the wicked being put into the hands of the righteous.

Four hundred years later, they rose up and called on the Lord of Sabaoth and said, "Give us what is owed us."

The latter rain is the blessing God is going to give to you, and it will be great. But what is your former rain? Get ready for your breakthrough. God is going to give you the former and the latter rain too. Look again at James 5:4. The Master Avenger is going to make sure you get paid back everything that should have already been yours but wasn't because your family didn't get its former rain. What does that mean?

If you are African American, many of your relatives didn't get paid what they should have because of the color of their skin. Whether your ancestors were slaves or whether they just didn't receive fair wages because of prejudice, you need to get excited. The Master Avenger is about to set the books straight. Everything your father should have had, everything your mother should have had, the wicked have stored up for in the last days (see James 5:3). Prosperity and abundance are promises to you by God. What's been stolen from you? Make a list and get excited.

Everything that has been stolen. Everything that your mother and father should have had. Anything your grandfather or your grandmother should have had. Anything that has been stolen. All of the former rain is being stored up and is about to be released on you, not only your latter rain, but your former rain also. Get ready for the window of heaven to open up and pour out such a blessing on you that you won't have room enough to receive it all.

Let's Remove the Curses and Release the Blessings on African Americans

As African Americans, begin to confess, with thanksgiving, calling on the Lord of Sabaoth, the Master Avenger. "Thank you," we cry out to the Master Avenger. "Start decree restoration. Everything that has been stolen from me, my mother and father, what they should have had. Everything that my grandmother and grandfather should have had that was stolen." All of the former rain is being stored up, so begin to release your faith on you now and your seed.

Cry out to the Master Avenger. "Give me what is owed to me now." Begin to cry out, "Please grant me favor. In Jesus' name." Now, let's remove the curses and release the blessings on African Americans.

Father, I come to you right now, in the name of Jesus. I come in agreement, with James and Betty Harvey, according to your Word and the blood of Jesus. I rebuke the curse and the spirit of poverty, lack, debt, and failure right now, and by the blood of Jesus shed through the crown of thorns, that curse is broken and reversed. I received everything that should have been in my family for generations. I receive now, the latter and the former rain. I receive prosperity and abundance in Jesus Christ. Amen.

CHAPTER 8

Conclusion

Sin is never fair, but it is predictable. Sins that are committed repeatedly are like weeds planted in the heart. You can mow them down, but, until they are understood and dealt with, they will crop back up. Iniquities are like the seeds of weeds—They may die as your forefathers have, but they will return the next year, or in this case, the next generation, whether they are planted by you, your parents, or your forefathers. The result is a crop of inherited weaknesses or family iniquities.

> As the bird by wandering, as the swallow
> by flying, so the curse causeless shall not come.
> (Proverbs 26:2, KJV)

> Thou shalt not bow down thyself to them,
> nor serve them: for I the Lord thy God am a
> jealous God, visiting the iniquity of the
> fathers upon the children unto third and
> fourth generation of them that hate me.
> (Exodus 20:5, KJV)

The law of iniquity states that the sins of the fathers will continue to the third and fourth generation for those who hate God. What about you and me who love God? For us, God has made a provision to reverse the curse of iniquities. Just as iniquities are passed through the bloodline, your exemption from the law of iniquities is through blood also. The blood sacrifice of your covenant with God.

In the old covenant that sacrifice was of bulls and goats, but in the new covenant, the perfect precious blood of Jesus cleansed you from sin and iniquity.

You no longer have to live bound by iniquities and generational curses and be defeated by sin because Jesus became both your "sin offering" and the "scapegoat" for your iniquities. His physical body was sacrificed and his perfect blood was offered to God for your sins and iniquities. He took our iniquities and buried them in the sea of forgetfulness. We now have something better than the types and shadows of the Old Testament. We have a better covenant in Jesus.

In the same way, after the supper he took the cup, saying, "This cup is the new covenant in my blood, which is poured out for you" (Luke 22:20, NIV). Jesus took on himself the curse of our iniquities. He became cursed so that we could be set free and be blessed. Christ hath redeemed us from the curse of the law, being made a curse for us: for it is written, cursed is every one that hangeth on a tree (Galatians 3:13, KJV).

The mystery of iniquity is already at work in our family bloodline. God is looking for true worshippers who are willing to become yielded vessels—so heaven can invade the earth. I am one voice, but if we, as Christians, will begin to repent for the iniquity that has crept into our families and our nation, God will cause the minds of his people to become right again. And, he will pour out his covenant blessings upon America. It is time to set the captives free, to conquer, possess, and to reign in all areas of our lives.

CHAPTER 9

Works Cited

King James Version, (KJV), King James Version Living Bible, The Message Remix Bible, The New American Bible (NAB), New Testament in Today's English, Amplified Bible, (Zondervan)

Brown, Rebecca, with Daniel Yoder. 1995. *Unbroken Curses.* Springdale, PA: Whitaker House. Chapter IV and Chapter VI (ISBN-088368-372-5). The use of personal items in satanic worship to send curses to people. Also, prayers to be released from it. I would like to personally thank Rebecca Brown and Daniel Yoder for all the time and insight on this topic concerning African Americans.

Hickey, Marilyn. 2008. *Blessing The Next Generation, FaithWorks.* Chapter III (ISBN-10: 0446699896).

Huch, Larry. 2004. *Free At Last.*

Huch, Larry. *Breaking the Cycle of Family Curses in the Year of 2000.* Tulsa, Oklahoma: Albury Publishing. Chapter VII (ISBN I-57778-124-4). I would like to thank Larry Huch for searching the Bible and gathering information concerning this topic on restoration. Also, the prayers for releasing the blessing, as well as showing the comparison of the children of Israel, when in slavery, and how African Americans were in slavery and when they were also cheated out of their wages.

Melba J. Duncan. *The Complete Idiot's Guide to African American History.* (Jim Crow Law) Chapter IV. Publisher: Alpha.

Melba J. Duncan. *The Complete Idiot's Guide to African American History.* (Lynch Willie, Speech) Chapter IV. Publisher: Alpha.

FOR CONFERENCE, REVIVAL, SPEAKING, PRAISE REPORTS

CONTACT: PASTOR JAMES HARVEY
(985) 222-0319 OR E-MAIL pastorjharvey@gmail.com